MW00652480

pictureshowpress.net

Cover image credit: Betsy Mars, Kingly Street Lights, London, 2017
Background image: mantinov, stock.adobe.com
Author photo credit: Stephen Howarth

FIRST EDITION

ISBN-13: 978-1-7324144-5-7
ISBN-10: 1-7324144-5-9

ALINEA

Betsy Mars

[signature: Betsy Mars]

Picture Show Press

Thank you for participating in the contest — I think it's such a fun event and enjoy getting to know the work of poets I haven't yet encountered. I hope you enjoy this book — my first "book child" so it holds a special place in my heart.
warm regards,
Betsy

Note: *Alinea* refers to the ¶, which indicates a new paragraph.

With enduring gratitude to my parents, David and Marien Mars.

POEMS

Synesthesia

In a state of brownie-found grace,
I lie bound to my bed, words trying to form
sentences, meaning
my words become pregnant
and I push, delivering them to the page.

Pastel iridescent ribbons
curl like kitetails in the flutter
of my mind, which names
it music and doesn't care when
sound becomes color.

At the Ob/Gyn

The doctor spreads a thin layer of conductive gel
on the moon-shaped surface of my pregnant skin.
The ultrasound wand passes over and detects a beat –
the faint first pulse of my new-formed boy –
the reality of a body within my body finally sinking in.

Across the street, my mother lies in intensive care,
paralyzed from an attempt to remove a tumor from her brain;

I encouraged the surgery. She might never walk again.
The doctor reads my tears as joy
and I couldn't say whether he's right or wrong.
It's true we're only flies to wanton gods –
we lay our eggs, create a buzz, and then we're gone.

When I was born

I was borne into a box
to warm my flesh –
they gave me heat
lamps to light the way.

An incubator to finish the task
my mother couldn't perform.
My premature body born,
small flesh untouched.

From a damp, dark world
of flesh and blood I was borne
into a box of warming lights,
swaddled in clean cotton

instead of womb. There was no
room to move when I was born,
the water breaking in the kitchen,
my mother washing at the sink.

She felt me sink toward the bottom
of her pelvic floor, held me tight
for hours while her body nurtured
mine a little more, grown impatient

I emerged and was borne
into a box, taken from her hands
and breast, lest I fail to thrive.

Sub Rosa

What's in a name? A tale of many things
past and present.
As it happens, when I think
I remember childhood taunts
and oft-told stories of
the origins of my names, juxtaposed:
On the one side,
a beloved grandmother/mother surrogate
and on the other, an incontinent doll, Betsy Wetsy.
A savior, a cow, and a seamstress
all merged together under pressure to form
a multifaceted but conflicted image of what a
Betsy was.
Davy Crockett's gun. The woman who nurtured
the woman who nurtured me. A magic bus.
Betsy was expected to be rejected
for my middle name, Andrea.
More sophisticated, I was told,
but also indicative of dysfunction:
a tribute to my mother's psychiatrist, André,
the man who nurtured the woman
who was neglected by her father
and rejected by her mother.
Not a common story in my white collar,
aerospace engineer, stay-at-home mom neighborhood.
What's in a name? A chocolate bar
by any other name would taste as sweet.
The sound of Marsbar was cloying
and repetitive, alternating with
allusions to little green men and Uranus,
such ridicule unanticipated by my grandfather

as he abandoned his unspellable, unacceptable
name at the entry point
by force or by choice in favor
of the simplicity and grace and unbloodied
history of Mars, the God of War.
What's in a name?
Had I arose by any other name, I would not be me.

In Tandem

The time had come to take the stand:
kicking it up and out of the way,
I wobbled from side to side
wearing my training wheels,
only just maintaining balance.

My father wrenched away my dependency.
Unbolted, I sat upright.
He kept a hand lightly on my back,
steadying, as I learned to ride alone.
Instead of unforgiving concrete, he gave me grass
to soften the blow: a lesson in man versus nature.

Wheels spinning, with effort I made my move.
Elation and premonition of the inevitable
separation as I rode free, relatively stable,
his imagined hand constant.

Over time along pitted paths, life's bumps and bruises
calloused my spirit, hardened my heart.
Obstinate and frightened, over time I rode alone;
bones brittle from frequent breaks
made future falls a risk.

When my father died, I clutched his life –
a comforting cardigan against my loss.
Now, beneath my wheels,
I feel the forgiving foundation.
I take the saddle again, this time in tandem,
I find my feet and go.

Letter to a Shipwreck

Obrigado my beached ship, *minha amiga.*
I am sorry you went down before delivering the loot.
I hope there was no life lost. Or party favors sullied.
I know you were carrying my birthday present —
the one I dropped long ago at 5 years old
(or possibly 6) in the streets of Rio —
the one that made up for the limbless beggars
and for the grassy knoll,
innocence flying away with the bird kites,
soaring.
Where is the walking My Size doll that was promised?
Where is the heart-shaped amethyst with its magic
clear purple protective powers?
Where is the white chocolate, in all its oxymoronic glory?
Where are the window stickers illuminating
brightly, like leaded glass gospel,
heaving?
Meu gato morreu. My bird has flown.
I am sure my ice cream cake has melted
in its confusion: Is it cake or is it ice cream?
and seeped through the hull,
running in delicious fingers to stroke the Amazon
where the piranha wait,
tasting the remains.

Driftwood

The wind chime pendulums
on the porch
were once tossed
driftwood on this beach –

here among the rocks and lost socks
and bits of sea glass
I wander the length of the shore
seeking the perfect shell –

to the right the sea grass waves
to the left small swells –
and in the distance
sailboats and kite surfers.

Instead I could sit still
on a square meter of beach
and find, if I look closely or dig
deep, every piece I seek –

the smooth stone perfect
to palm or skim across calm waters,
the rough rock with striations
like rainbows, the abandoned
shell once home to dinner,
the glass shard of a bottle
that held minerals and sugar –
sun and soil magic for the tongue
in grief or celebration,

or solace on a lonely night
when I try to sort, seeking
home in a handful of beach.

Armario

Delicate spoons with round silver bowls – *cruzeiros* –
little pitchforks, and knives encrusted with miniscule
bejeweled pomegranates –

your drawers held linens, magic, tiny utensils
decorated with gems and smooth, cool stones –
small even in my child's hand,
fit only for fairies –
so exquisite that I couldn't imagine what purpose they served.

The *Cumaru* panels breathe,
cinnamon scent from Rio,
a whiff of my childhood home.
Delicacies
I have hidden in your upper cabinet –
I was so small, waiting – hoping – to be found.

My mother's essential oils shine in your wooden luster.
My father's salt rubbed wounds in your tarnished handles.
My memories fold like your doors,
hinging back, revealing.

Aromatherapy

for my mother

Hanging empty in the closet are the outlines of
the physical reality of you.
Frequently worn items spared or
not yet relinquished
to moths or Goodwill. Just
your size, your style,
the outer shell of the outer you.
If I hold them up to my ear, will I hear the sea?
If I could fill them – especially
that purple ultrasuede coat that was custom made
for you –
would your earthly body return?

A few bottles of your nail polish solidify
in the medicine cabinet. Your favorite colors.
One last effort to maintain control
over one aspect of your beauty that the cancer
(which took your hair, bloated you,
took away your bladder control, and your lovely legs)
could not destroy.
The pull of the bed finally
caused your muscles and organs to atrophy but
your nails were your domain.

Mostly – most importantly – the remains of
a bottle of French perfume
that was your staple when I was small
and you were
an impossibly beautiful scented goddess

and I was my truer self.
In awe of you always, one whiff upon cracking open
the cracking box is all it takes to reconnect
me with you, with me
as I ride home to myself on
an evaporating trail of fumes.

Sillage

I dream of genie, on a trail of vapors
you come, as I crack open the cracked box –
I slip through a scented wormhole of space
and time to the heart of the matter.

In another dimension, I follow close behind
on the essence of you – the base notes
left in the bottle.
My conscious mind amnesiac,
but my primitive nose remembers.
Scent remains unperturbed.
A complex perfume, imported,
outlasting you and your body –
French, at your service, no memorial
except your legacy of language and luxury.

The box sits on the shelf, idle, until I need you;
and then, with one whiff I follow,
transported to a splintered realm –
wholey, holey, Holy.
Shadowed and strung with trip wires:
nurture and neglect, ice and fire.
Memories dissipate like a genie
after three wishes are spent.

My first wish and only wish would be that
this fragrance lingers until I too depart,
leaving my own olfactory trace in my wake.
The bottle tightly stoppered to preserve
my mothered memories perfumed –
only the best notes remain.

Ode to a mouse

I socked him away,
safe from escape,
with warmth
to the touch and softness –
smelling of mouse
pellets and hay.

Like a lucky rabbit foot
to stroke in the night
when demons came
calling for me, he comforted,
but I slept right through
to the mourning –
he was cold
and hard to the touch.

In my guilt, I emptied
the sock and left him
rigid in the cage,
to be discovered
and buried,
along with my memory
of inadvertent, mindless murder.

At eight years old,
I learned that love could be lethal.

What is essential

Your honey ears perk up as I read you
The Little Prince; like the fox you know
language is the source of misunderstandings.
You sniff and lick instead, your tongue velvet –
like rose petals – your teeth thorns,
poised to protect.

You know better than to seek admiration
or count stars like currency;
you get drunk on games of fetch,
know day from night
without the benefit of lamplight.

You understand the necessity
of keeping the baobabs at bay
and raking out the volcanos –
even the ones that might be extinct.
You dig out roots in the yard
and rake the carpet into submission.

We have our rites and our rituals.
I have walked and watered you.
You warm my feet at night.
You have tamed me and wait
patiently while I am taken
away by a migration of wild birds.

In the end, you pull me back,
a well singing to my soul:
she loves me, she loves me.

A Short Half-Life

Trickling tears well up
 from some dire place –
a hint of a headache
nags at the back of the
serotonin control center,
the receptor gates raised with the blood waters –
with the ebb and flow
of the chemical mix
of the unbalanced psyche.
I reach for an explanation and find it
in the still-snapped compartment
of my daily dosage:
the remains of a pill, forgotten in the morning rush
until the reawakening of the sleeping
black dog that claws at my raw edges.

Reparations

Such a fine web you strung:
light lines in my window
I didn't see. I didn't see
when I pushed
my hand through,
expecting the resistance
of glass. I punched
a hole mindless
of your efforts and you.
You patiently re-hung,
thread
after thread,
I watched you return
to the center time
and again until at last
it was complete
and you rested, well-earned.
In the morning,
tatters of silk blown out in the night.

If I were free of gravity

If I were a rich man, I'd play the fiddle on the roof
like a floating violinist in a painting by Chagall.
I'd elevate myself
above everybody else.
I'd tune out the world, ignoring change,
and live in my cocoon until ready to emerge,
weaving silk from my salivary glands.

Eating the finest mulberry leaves,
I'd live in a cloistered world,
important and cultivated –
white naked vulnerable, tiny horns on my back.

Flightless, I'd depend on humans for my brief survival.
Inside my cocoon, I'd thread my prism's bars.
Mission accomplished,
I'll be dipped in boiling water
to make my silken treasure easier to unravel.
The world outside revels in my sputum,
dyeing for its glorious sheen and strength.

Feeling the fire rising,
I'd break my bonds and escape
through a hole of my own making,
turn a new leaf and fly off gently
to the waking moon.
There, alight and in tune,
I'd land in lunar dust
with delicate feet and
plant my silken flag.

4 a.m. Sorting Game

At 4 a.m. the dog's panting
and the hamster on the wheel
can sound the same,
and my brain has to sort
to determine if it's pain
or pent up energy at play
before I can sleep again –
one is a labor of life,
the other a labor of breath –
and all I can think either way,
how imminent is death.

David: Decline and Fall

for my stepmother

1

As long as you are there
so is he, my father-home.
I can still find the places he remains
in memory.

In the chair, doing the crossword puzzle
in pen, listening to Mozart,
watching the daily passing parade of pelicans
returning to their nests at dusk.

He still has a place at the table –
close to the kitchen, not far to stumble.
Still there like the blood stain on the rug,
when he hit his head,
no one told me.

There is the imprint of the hospital bed
where we bathed him
with tenderness and dismay,
and he endured it, stoic.

There he is each July
on the balcony, tequila in hand,
gleeful at each burst of blossoming light,
the light of the party.

Still there, storytelling and sharing bawdy jokes,
pouring tart wine, passing stinky cheeses.
Giddy as the full moon rise
and fades – as you leave.

2

I came back to find you
in that room where the curtain separated
you from your neighbor, Spanish soaps blaring,
daylight stabilizing,
the moving walls cast shadows
changing before your eyes
oxygen deprived
sharing fearful dreams of persecution:

Gas chambers, six-pointed yellow
star pinned to your
hospital gown open, exposed
holding the hand of your granddaughter,
your progeny, your hope
your mind lurching to a stop
like a car running out of gas
and stuck in the rut of your fears.

Potholes

After a winter of hard weather,
the road ahead lies pitted –
pocked by cold and heaviness –
small depressions to catch a tire,
or a tired traveller too weary
to veer, bleary-eyed and maybe
indifferent by now.
Spring water pools in the wells
formed when the smooth
surface cracks – still water
reflecting new green trees,
the sky above, the moving truck
bearing down in the middle distance.

Post-Mortem

I wrote through the mourning,
the grieving, identifying –
the body cold
in need of warming.

The tea gone cold
upon the table
his body, her body –
anybody would have failed

to recognize the end
was coming and there was nothing
to do nothing in retrospect
was all I could do

so now there's the writing –
the obituary, the morgue,
the questions that linger
as you, or you, stare from the page,
pointing your finger.

Incarnation

for Charles

> *"... All poets*
> *understand the final uselessness of words...."* ~ Joy Harjo

In my dream you were reborn –
playing under shading palm fronds
in some island jungle I recognized you,

your toes sunk in the loamy earth.
You were foreign and your tongue
no longer knew my name.

You used coconuts for cricket balls,
Your name meant tea.
You were a child, I was still me.

You were lost to me for a time
in a place I couldn't reach,
your body freshly formed.

Youtopia

My perfect journey: headless.
Heedless of my thoughts, mindful and mindless.
No shoulds or woulds. No sense of unworthiness.
No thought for things done, or not done, or undone.

Strolling through places of beauty sublime,
greenest meadows or fern-floored forests,
leading to peat-filled distilleries where they make
small batches of nectar, transcendent
on craggy outcrops at the end of continents,
with no risk of falling off. No acrophobia or claustrophobia.
No phobia. Safe treks down dry-boned paths
littered with shards of domestic pottery
where the volcano blew
        Life in pieces.

Or time travel to the past, clearing dark places
mined with trigger spots and wrongdoings:
Poorly handled breakups or ill-advised makeups,
child-rearing disasters: the nucleus of neurotic reactors,
defused.

Then celebratory trips to champagne caves, riding on riverboats
where movement and stillness coexist. Sober and intoxicated,
as the bank flows by. Or through Rousseau jungles
plentiful with beasts and wildness.
Safari tents are filled with soft scents and the sense of being
embodied in a distant place where light doesn't leach
away the black from the sky,
and the vast spread of stars is revealed,
terrifying, humbling, and alive.

Canvassing Paris

What I have seen in Paris:
exposed beams, crumbling concrete,
bony streets knobbed with good intentions.

So many beginnings, imagined middles,
to unimagined ends.
Pathways meander to more pathways –

shops and shops of shabby memorabilia,
cheaply celebrating history –
L'Histoire, La Gloire –
rolled like flaked chocolate

around the meringue ball of the city:
its shell after shell of deliciousness
and bitterness, of cakes and prison breaks,

deportation and occupation. Absinthe-
drenched and sun-bleached, speckled
picnickers on pointillist blankets

eating *foie gras* and playing *paté* cake
they flirt and give way to *gendarmes*
and Fauvism. The raw heart of the city given up

to the eagle-eyed and sad
among us. We devour it, arteries
and all, hoping to feel the blood-
cheap cognac, hot in our veins.

Love Train

You're a dream of a cat:
a rising and falling orange
cream-colored cloud
of perfection, a confection
of belly rumbling pleasure,
making fast tracks
as you stroke through my hair;
your breath warm in my ear
speaks comforting nothings,
paw on my neck, secure,
and securing me in my place –
graceful whiskers gently binding,
sandwiched between my pillow, your head.

Creature Comforts

If I could talk to the animals
I'd gather creatures all around me;
carrying them catlike in my mouth
softly communicating
through touch, telepathy, or teeth –

Or birdlike, feather my arms with amethyst
and join the formation with wings,
strung out v-shaped.
We'd band together safely,
each in our proper place, flying but not in flight.

I'd blow the top off my head and spout
my presence high into the air, grow gills
and breathe underwater... and slowly...
I'd practice bubble communication
and learn to whistle beyond human earshot.

On soft cat feet, my tell-tale tail swishing
and back arched, I'd raise my hackles
to warn predators and rivals
to keep their distance.
In a low growl, my throat would rumble my displeasure.

In a dog-eat-dog ass-sniffing world
my every inhale would be endlessly informative,
odors wafting through my synapses
triggering unarticulated volumes
received in a few twitches of a nose.

If I could talk to the animals
I could rest easy knowing that the Great Pink Sea Snail
would not be a-salted and the Pushmi-pullyu,
like me, would finally find its direction.
My kingdom would have no bounds.

ACKNOWLEDGMENTS

I know this threatens to be longer than my book, but since it is my first chapbook, forgive me for going overboard in my exuberance. I am filled with gratitude.

Thank you to all who have helped and encouraged me. I hope you know how much I value you, my longtime friends as well as some whom I have never met in "real" life. You are the family I have chosen.

After my parents to whom this book is dedicated, going chronologically, I owe a debt of gratitude to Raundi Moore-Kondo for first publishing my poetry in her anthology, *A Poet Is A Poet No Matter How Small*. That first step gave me a taste of possibility.

Stephen Howarth believed in the value of my writing and helped cultivate it and support me through my early (and ongoing) sense of inadequacy, and the overwhelming task of finding my voice, my place, and my community. His willingness to work with me via Skype in the early hours of his day with good humor and respect for my instincts has been invaluable.

To Donna Hilbert who invited me into her workshop fold where she and my fellow poets have been unerring sources of wisdom, poetic knowledge and inspiration, and often kind critics when I have needed some objectivity.

Through Donna, I met Shannon Phillips, who has generously and patiently guided me through this process and who, for some inexplicable reason, wanted to make me a book. She has been a godsend.

My stepmother, Joan Banes, and my children, Daniel and Kat, have given me love, support (or tolerance), and often a kind of expansion through their mind-broadening thoughts and love of language. I would be remiss if I did not acknowledge my dog and cats, who provide so much comfort and diversion when I get too far inside my head.

Lastly, I want to thank Emily Dickinson whose rhythms and words resounded in my 16 year-old head and heart, and e.e. cummings who showed me how poetry can be both fun and deep. Joni Mitchell, too, who to my mind is a supreme poet, and whose music and lyrics are so true and graceful, and have left an imprint of song in my subconscious.

Grateful acknowledgments to the publications in which these poems previously appeared:

Anti-Heroin Chic ("Synesthesia"); *Cadence Collective* ("Ode to a mouse"); *The California Quarterly* ("Incarnation"); *The Fox Poetry Box* ("Incarnation"); *Intersections, ZzyZx WriterZ* ("David: Decline and Fall"); *A Poet is a Poet No Matter How Tall, Episode II: Attack of the Poems,* For the Love of Words (Press) ("Aromatherapy"); *Postcard Poems and Prose* ("Potholes"); *Red Wolf Journal* ("Armario" and "What is essential"); *Redshift* ("A Letter to a Shipwreck"); *Sheila-Na-Gig* ("Canvassing Paris"); *Silver Birch Press* ("Creature Comforts," "If I were free of gravity," "In Tandem," "Sillage," "Sub Rosa," and "Youtopia"); and *Writing In A Woman's Voice* ("Aromatherapy," "A Short Half-Life," "Sillage," and "Sub Rosa").

Made in the USA
Columbia, SC
24 June 2022

62205320R00024